Whale Watching

Josephine Croser   Veronica Jefferis

Each winter a whale comes to our bay.

I stand on the sand
and watch the whale in the water.

Sometimes I wonder where
it has been.

Perhaps it has been to Antarctica.

Sometimes I wonder what it has seen.

Perhaps it has seen shipwrecks . . .

and mountains beneath the waves.

Perhaps it has seen sharks
and killer whales.

I like watching the whale as it swims.

I like seeing the spray in the air
when it blows . . .

and hearing the whack of its flippers
on the water.

Sometimes I wonder why the whale leaps so high.

Perhaps it is watching me!

First Published by Era Publications,
220 Grange Road, Flinders Park, South Australia 5025

Text Copyright © Josephine Croser, 1995
Illustrations by Veronica Jefferis
Copyright © Era Publications, 1995
Printed in Hong Kong
First Published 1996

**National Library of Australia
Cataloguing-in-Publication Data:**
Croser, Josephine, 1943-
     Whale Watching

          ISBN 1 86374 240 9 (Small Bk.).
          ISBN 1 86374 245 X (Big Bk.).

          1. Readers - Whales. 2. Readers (Primary). I.
          Jefferis, Veronica. II. Title. (Series : Magic bean).

428.6

Available in:

Australia from Era Publications, 220 Grange Road,
Flinders Park, South Australia 5025

Canada from Vanwell Publishing Ltd, 1 Northrup Cresc., PO Box 2131, Stn B,
St Catharines, ONT L2M 6P5

New Zealand from Reed Publishing, 39 Rawene Road,
Birkenhead, Auckland 10

Singapore, Malaysia & Brunei from Publishers Marketing Services
Pty Ltd, 10-C Jalan Ampas, #07-01 Ho Seng Lee Flatted Warehouse, Singapore 1232

United Kingdom from Heinemann Educational Publishers,
Halley Court, Jordan Hill, Oxford OX2 8EJ

United States of America from Australian Press ™,
c/- Ed-Tex, 15235 Brand Blvd, #A107, Mission Hills CA 91345